D1361112

SNAKES ALIVE

Rattlesnakes

by Colleen Sexton

BELLWETHER MEDIA • MINNEAPOLIS, MN

Note to Librarians, Teachers, and Parents:

Blastoff! Readers are carefully developed by literacy experts and combine standards-based content with developmentally appropriate text.

Level 1 provides the most support through repetition of high-frequency words, light text, predictable sentence patterns, and strong visual support.

Level 2 offers early readers a bit more challenge through varied simple sentences, increased text load, and less repetition of high-frequency words.

Level 3 advances early-fluent readers toward fluency through increased text and concept load, less reliance on visuals, longer sentences, and more literary language.

Level 4 builds reading stamina by providing more text per page, increased use of punctuation, greater variation in sentence patterns, and increasingly challenging vocabulary.

Level 5 encourages children to move from "learning to read" to "reading to learn" by providing even more text, varied writing styles, and less familiar topics.

Whichever book is right for your reader, Blastoff! Readers are the perfect books to build confidence and encourage a love of reading that will last a lifetime!

This edition first published in 2010 by Bellwether Media, Inc.

No part of this publication may be reproduced in whole or in part without written permission of the publisher. For information regarding permission, write to Bellwether Media, Inc., Attention: Permissions Department, 5357 Penn Avenue South, Minneapolis, MN 55419.

Library of Congress Cataloging-in-Publication Data

Sexton, Colleen.
 Rattlesnakes / by Colleen Sexton.
   p. cm. – (Blastoff! readers. Snakes alive!)
 Summary: "Simple text and full-color photography introduce beginning readers to rattlesnakes. Developed by literacy experts for students in kindergarten through third grade"–Provided by publisher.
 Includes bibliographical references and index.
 ISBN 978-1-60014-319-9 (hardcover : alk. paper)
 1. Rattlesnakes–Juvenile literature. I. Title.
 QL666.O69S49 2010
 597.96'38–dc22
                          2009037595

Text copyright © 2010 by Bellwether Media, Inc.
Printed in the United States of America, North Mankato, MN.

010110   1149

Contents

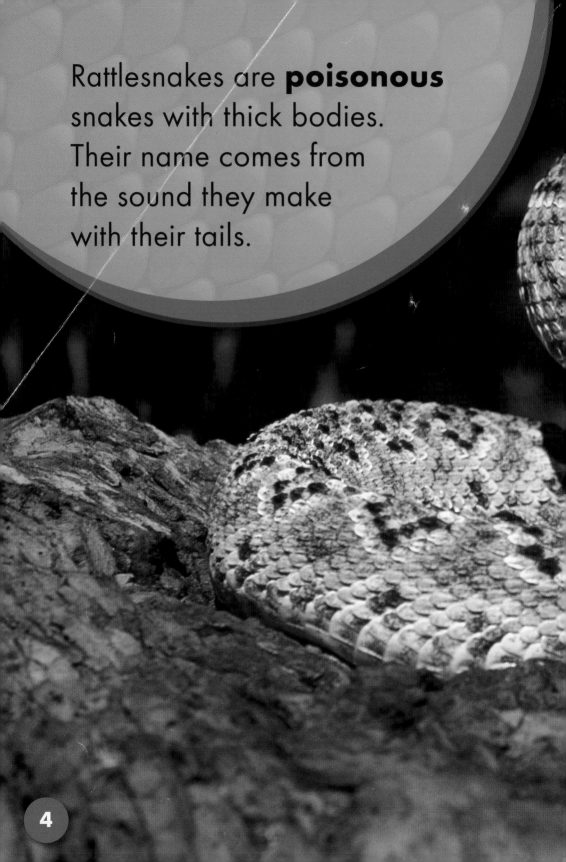

Rattlesnakes are **poisonous** snakes with thick bodies. Their name comes from the sound they make with their tails.

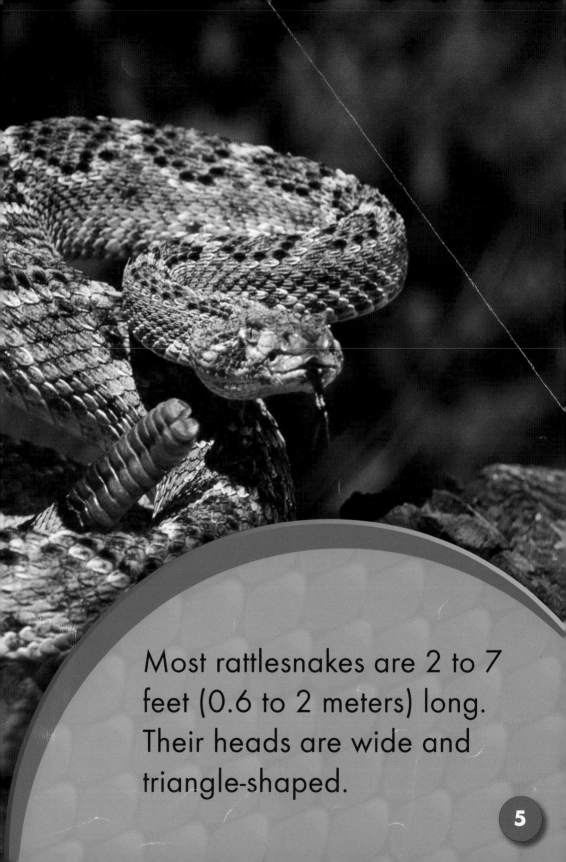

Most rattlesnakes are 2 to 7 feet (0.6 to 2 meters) long. Their heads are wide and triangle-shaped.

Rattlesnakes are brown or gray. They have diamond shapes, spots, and stripes on their backs. Their bellies are cream-colored.

The colors and shapes are **camouflage**. Rattlesnakes look like the patterns that sunlight and shadows make on the ground.

Rattlesnakes have dry skin covered with **scales**. The scales on their backs are small.

The large scales on their bellies are called **scutes**. These grab on to the ground and help rattlesnakes move forward.

scutes

= areas where rattlesnakes live

Rattlesnakes live
in North America,
Central America,
and South America.

They live in deserts, marshes, and grasslands.

Rattlesnakes grow throughout their lives. They **shed** their skin whenever it gets too tight.

A rattlesnake's tail has a **rattle**.
A new piece of the rattle is
added each time the rattlesnake
sheds its skin.

rattle

The hard pieces of
the rattle fit together
loosely. They make
a buzzing sound
when the rattlesnake
shakes its tail.

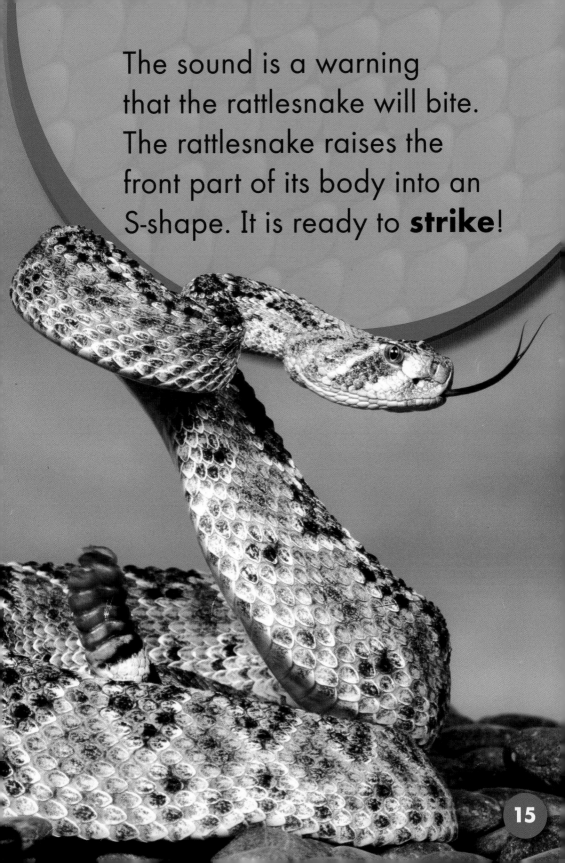

The sound is a warning that the rattlesnake will bite. The rattlesnake raises the front part of its body into an S-shape. It is ready to **strike**!

The rattle's sound does not
scare away hawks, coyotes,
roadrunners, and other **predators**
that hunt rattlesnakes.

Rattlesnakes are predators too. They stay still. They wait for birds, rats, and other small **prey**.

pits

Rattlesnakes have two **pits** on their heads that sense heat. They let rattlesnakes find prey that have **body temperatures** warmer than the air.

Rattlesnakes bite their prey with sharp **fangs**. The fangs unfold from the backs of the mouths.

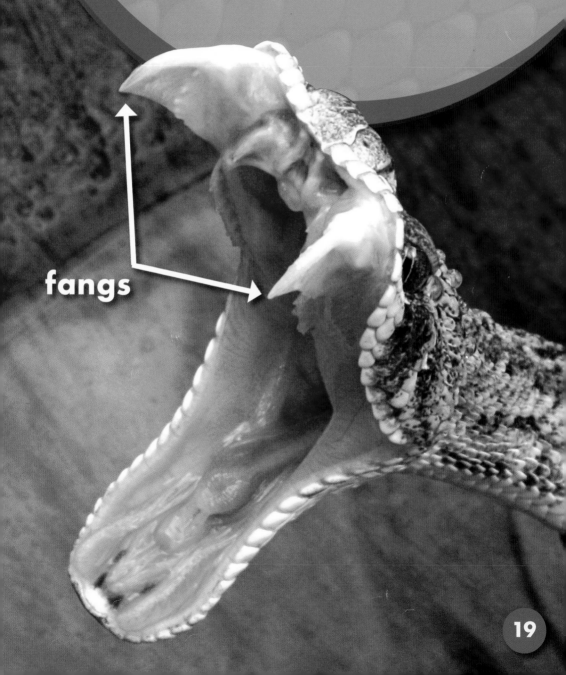

fangs

The fangs are hollow. A poison called **venom** flows through the fangs and into the bite.

venom

The venom makes animals stop breathing and die. Rattlesnakes then stretch their jaws wide and swallow their prey whole!

Glossary

body temperature—the amount of heat in an animal's body

camouflage—coloring and patterns that hide an animal by making it look like its surroundings

fangs—sharp, curved teeth; rattlesnakes have hollow fangs through which venom can move into a bite.

pits—areas of a snake's face that sense the body heat of an animal; pits tell a snake where an animal is and its size.

poisonous—able to kill or harm with a poison; the venom that a rattlesnake makes is a poison.

predator—an animal that hunts other animals for food

prey—an animal hunted by another animal for food

rattle—hard pieces at the end of a rattlesnake's tail that fit together; the rattle makes a buzzing sound when a rattlesnake shakes its tail.

scales—small plates of skin that cover and protect a snake's body

scutes—large scales on the belly of a snake that are attached to muscles; snakes use scutes to move from place to place.

shed—to let something fall off; snakes rub their bodies against rocks or trees to help shed their skin.

strike—to quickly throw the head and front part of the body at a predator or prey

venom—a poison that some snakes make; rattlesnake venom is deadly.

To Learn More

AT THE LIBRARY
Fiedler, Julie. *Rattlesnakes*. New York, N.Y.:
PowerKids Press, 2008.

Gibbons, Gail. *Snakes*. New York, N.Y.: Holiday
House, 2007.

Gunzi, Christiane. *The Best Book of Snakes*. New
York, N.Y.: Kingfisher, 2003.

ON THE WEB
Learning more about rattlesnakes
is as easy as 1, 2, 3.

1. Go to www.factsurfer.com.

2. Enter "rattlesnakes" into the search box.

3. Click the "Surf" button and you will see a list of
   related Web sites.

With factsurfer.com, finding more information is just a
click away.

Index

The images in this book are reproduced through the courtesy of: Ron Kimball/Kimballstock, front cover, pp. 4-5, 14-15; Rusty Dodson, pp. 6-7; Jack Milchanowski, p. 7 (small); Lori Skelton, p. 8; Rolf Nussbaumer, p. 9; Jon Eppard, p. 10 (small); Juan Martinez, pp. 10-11, 17; McDonald Wildlife Photog./Animals Animals – Earth Scenes, p. 12; Steve Byland, p. 13; Kitchin/Hurst, p. 14 (small); Kim Taylor/naturepl.com, p. 16; Michael Weber, p. 18; Audrey Snider-Bell, p. 19; National Geographic/Getty Images, p. 20 (small); John Cancalosi, pp. 20-21.